truth
be told
quotes

wisdom
for real life

By Colleen Doyle Bryant

To all my teachers,
Thank you.

Published by LoveWell Press
LoveWellPress.com

Explore free learning resources at
TruthBeToldQuotes.com

Truth Be Told Quotes, Third Edition
Copyright © 2022 by Colleen Doyle Bryant.

Published in USA
Originally published 2018.
Imagery revised in 2020 and 2022.

Print book ISBN: 979-8-9867776-1-0
ebook ISBN: 979-8-9867776-2-7

Contents

Making mistakes is part of growing up.

Just try to make the kind your family can laugh about over holiday dinner.

Young people are supposed to do some stupid stuff, right? It's part of being young. What you want are the youthful adventures that will be embarrassingly rehashed over holiday dinners for years to come.

Like that story about your uncle with the goat, the bubble wrap, and the ill-timed dare. Your mom always rolls her eyes and looks disapproving, but she's chuckling on the inside.

Some mistakes can cause life-altering damage. Those mistakes will get you pursed lips and disapproving glares. So ask yourself before you leap... how will this story play at dinner in a few years?

The secret to success isn't just doing what you love.

It's finding something you are interested in, and then working to be good at it.

It's great if you can find the perfect job that lights your interest and comes to you naturally. But realistically, few people have their dream job on day one. Getting to do what you love in the future starts with finding a balance between your abilities, your interests, and your work ethic.

Find something you have the ability to be good at, are interested in doing, and are willing to work for.

It's like you have adjustment levels... if your ability is low, turn up the work ethic to get better at it. If the work isn't interesting right now, know that slogging through the boring stuff is turning up your abilities. Eventually you'll find the sweet spot where ability and interest make it easy to work hard.

Sometimes you need to choose to do things you don't want to do.

Just remember your reasons for choosing.

Here's a wonderfully liberating secret... you don't "have to" do anything. Even though you may not enjoy some of the stuff you choose to do, you still get to make the choice.

Take homework—you do it because you want grades that will lead to future opportunities. Job starts at 6am? You choose to get up early so you'll get paid.

You may want to blow off your responsibilities to create an obstacle course for your pet llama. But instead, you choose to prioritize the tasks that help you get other things you want.

Feeling like a victim of all the things you think you "have to" do will really drag you down. Instead, consider what benefit you are giving yourself—opportunity, approval, money. The choices and the rewards are yours.

"Sure. Ok, boss."

What could these simple words mean? Maybe they mean, "Sure. I'm totally ok staying late Friday night to sort the recyclable cans by color." Or maybe it was more like, "Sure. Okaaay. I'll sort the cans. But not without letting you know I think you're a total scobberlotcher."

Tone and body language speak volumes. And sometimes, we use them to make our displeasure known. It can feel good to win back a sense of power by delivering the words we "should" say along with an annoyed tone or eye roll. But even this lubberwort of a boss knows her employee just tried to put her down. Most people don't take kindly to that. And sometimes, it's downright counterproductive.

What you say matters as much as how you say it. When you treat others with respect, you're a lot more likely to get the respect you want in return. And even if your boss doesn't stop acting like a gnashnab, you can feel pride in your heart for setting the right example.

You are connected
to a family,
a community,
a world.

Use your power wisely.

You have tremendous power. Everything you do sets off a cascade of ripple effects that impacts your family, your community, your world. It's pretty amazing when you think about it.

Some actions set off rolling waves of goodness that raise up those around you. Some actions set off a tsunami that swamps others in the lumpy sewage of your consequences.

In every careless or thoughtful act, you are the master of your universe. What kind of waves do you want to create?

Keep your lessons.

Let go of your scars.

Make tomorrow a new day.

Stuff happens—icky, painful, embarrassing stuff. Maybe a presentation goes badly even though you worked hard. Maybe it goes terribly because you *didn't* work hard. Maybe that presentation is why you'll live in infamy for the great hamster debacle.

But it's precisely those challenging moments that give us opportunities to learn something and to grow.

When one of life's tough lessons has you down, you can wallow in it. Or, you can keep the lesson, let go of the scar, and make tomorrow a new day.

You don't have to like what happened, but you can find a way to learn from it and to live differently after it.

And by the way, no one else is sitting around, their mind on a repeat loop, reliving the hamster debacle, over and over and over. You probably don't need to either.

There's the easy way,

and the right way.

It's easy to hear what you want to hear. It's easy to hurry through a job done poorly. It's easy to blame someone else. But the easy way is only easy for a little while.

Over time, easy outs and half measures cause a never-ending, nagging pain, like a splinter that reminds you with every step that it's still annoyingly embedded in your left butt cheek.

Doing something the right way—in a relationship, for your future, at your job—might be harder at first, but at least the splinter is out, and your left butt cheek will thank you.

If you want to come home, slip into fuzzy socks, microwave some cabbage rolls, and binge watch a zorbing tournament, that's cool. You be you.

But it's not ok for people to use "well that's just the way I am" as an excuse to be tone deaf to the impact they have on other people.

"You be you" is about respecting each other's uniqueness. It's not permission to roll over other people, even if they are a zorbing champion.

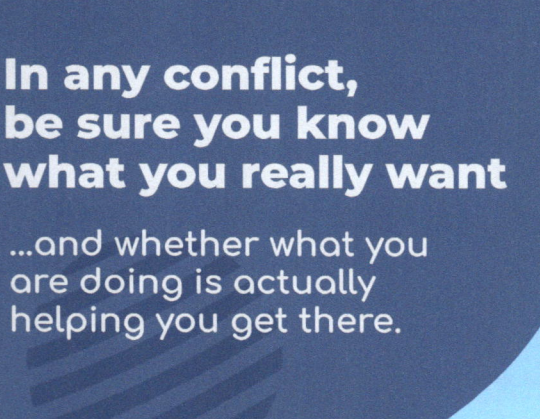

**In any conflict,
be sure you know
what you really want**

...and whether what you
are doing is actually
helping you get there.

Whether it's a friend, a boss, an obtuse government... everyone has an issue with someone at some point. Whatever your conflict is about, personal attacks and overreaction won't help resolve it.

Instead, ask yourself what you really want, and whether the way you are handling the situation will get you there. Do you want an apology? Acknowledgment? Change?

Whatever it is, you're a lot more likely to get what you want if you stay focused with actions that can actually help.

Everybody feels bad sometimes. In fact sometimes, you're supposed to feel bad.

Like when you bumped into that guy and he spilled Starbucks all over his mom? That bad feeling was empathy—and it means you're compassionate.

Or that time you did that totally embarrassing thing we swore never to mention? That bad feeling was appropriate shame, and it'll keep you from running around howling narwhal mating calls so you can "feel like a unicorn of the sea." (Again.)

And that time you felt terrible about lying? That was your conscience and it'll help you remember to be a person you can be proud of.

Now sometimes, we feel bad about things we don't really need to. If you're beating yourself up for something that wasn't wrong or harmful, you may be ok just letting that go. And if you can't stop feeling bad even though you try, it's ok to ask for help.

The great thing about growing up is you get to manage your own life.

The bad thing about growing up is you need to manage your own life.

One of the best parts of becoming a young adult is the freedom to stretch your wings. But one of the hardest things about becoming a young adult is that your freedom requires responsibility. If you want to soar, it's up to you to look after yourself and to make choices that will keep you on your path.

So, when it gets hard to keep doing the responsible thing, remember why you're doing it—for your own quality of life and your goals. You are the boss of you and you're starting to set your own course.

Oh and by the way, the more you establish a reputation for being trustworthy, the more freedom you'll have to explore. And nothing feels quite like reaching a new waypoint on your journey knowing you earned it yourself.

You know how your conscience makes you feel awful when you make a bad choice, even if no one else knows about it? It just follows you around, poking at your heart, giving you the stink eye. Poke. Poke.

That same conscience can make you feel great when you make a good choice, even if no one else knows about it.

When you choose to be kind, responsible, or honest, your conscience is there to swell your heart with pride and fill you with good vibes.

If you find yourself wondering what's in it for you to do the right thing, let your conscience be your guide. Because positive vibes beat stink eye any day.

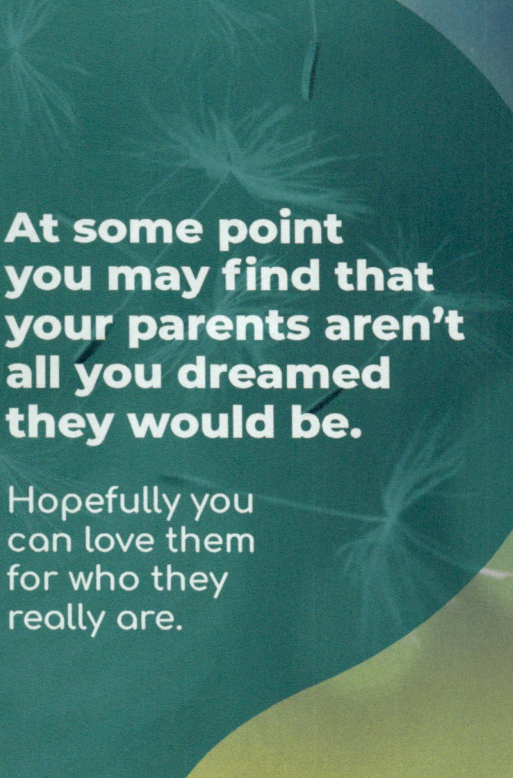

At some point you may find that your parents aren't all you dreamed they would be.

Hopefully you can love them for who they really are.

Before you were born, your parents had dreams about who you'd be. As it turns out, you're your own person, with your own personality. ("I want to do contact juggling, not ballet, Dad!") And they had to learn to accept you for who you really are.

There's going to come a time when you look at your parents and you might be disappointed that they aren't all you dreamed they would be.

Just like you, your parents are who they are, with their own baggage that helped make them that way. They probably made some very human mistakes. And there's a good chance that they did what they thought was best at the time. Hopefully you can find a way to love them for who they are, not who you wished they would be.

Life is about relationships—at home, at work, in your community. And relationships require give and take. Just because you can do something, doesn't mean it's fair or kind or honest or responsible.

You could use your age, size and wickedly clever mind to fleece those naïve eight-year-olds out of their lemonade-stand money.
But should you?

You could pile your four best friends and a slobbering Saint Bernard into your grandma's Mini Cooper for an epic road trip.
But should you?

There are plenty of things you might be able to get away with, but at what cost to your relationships or your sense of self? Be the kind of person you'd like to see looking back at you.

**Take joy
in others' joy,**

and you get
joy to infinity

No doubt being on the receiving end of good things makes you feel like a winner. But what about when other people get something they want—a good grade, a new opportunity, praise? Does their win, by default, make you a loser? Of course not.

Someone else's success doesn't have to be your failure. The fact that your sister got inducted into the Bossaball Hall of Fame doesn't have to be about you at all.

At a minimum, you're denying yourself a lot of opportunities to share in some joy. Think about it... if you're only happy at your own success, you only get to be joyful when you do something great.

But if you share your best friends', colleagues', even your sister's joy when they do well, you get joy to infinity.

There's no road to happiness.

It's more of a winding path through hills and valleys.

In the end, it's the journey that matters.

Ever notice how obsessed we are with finding happiness? Like there's a map with turn-by-turn directions to a place called "Happiness."

Maybe it'd be better to shut off the nav and enjoy some side trips up peaks and down valleys, into joys and sorrows, passing through disappointments and emerging into renewed hopes.

In the end, all those little ups and downs are what keep the journey interesting and keep us growing into our best selves.

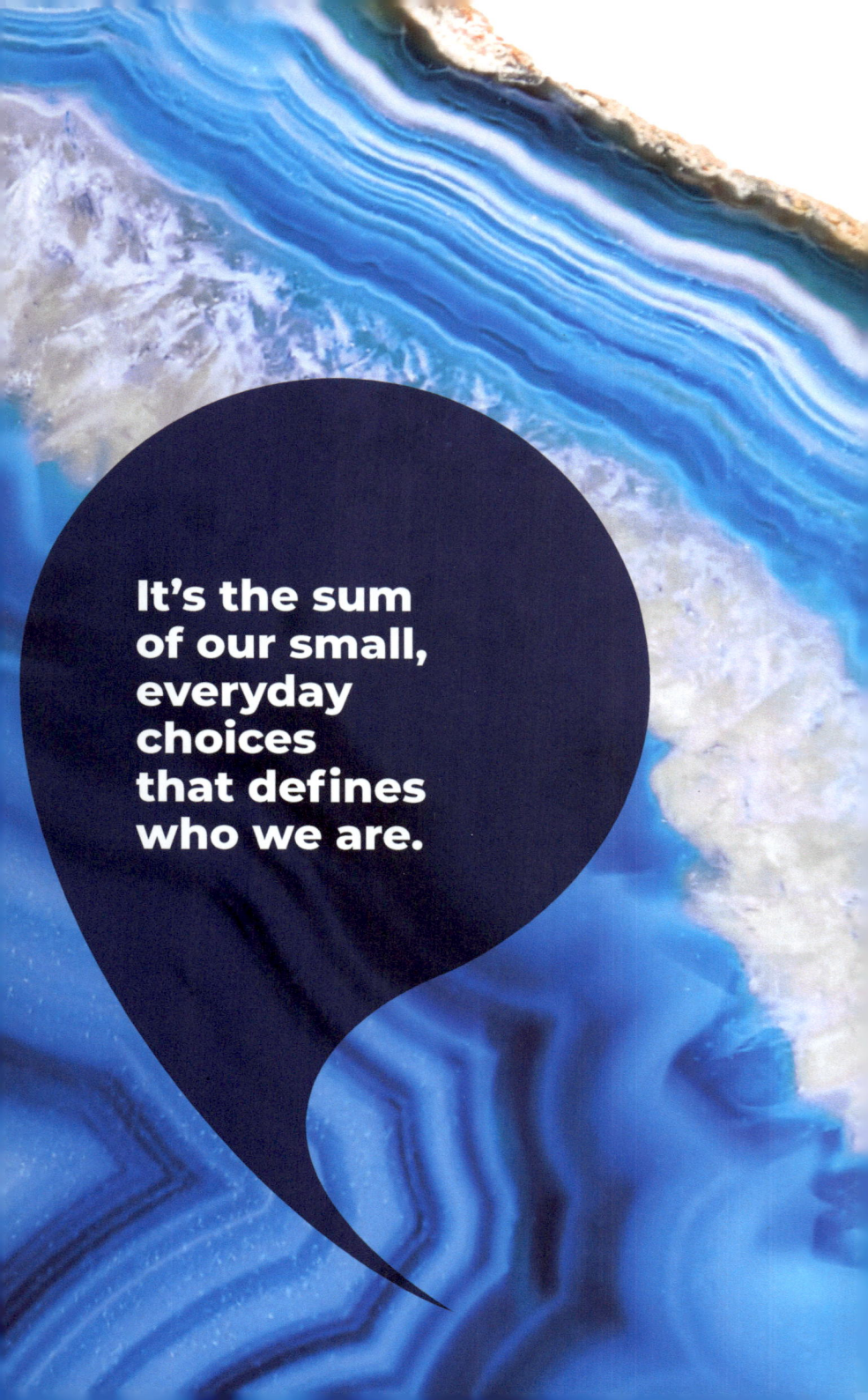

It's the sum of our small, everyday choices that defines who we are.

Most of life is a series of little choices that add up to define the type of person you are. In a given moment, should you be honest or bend the truth? Throw shade or be respectful? Blow off your responsibilities or do what you say you'll do?

The moments that define who you are usually aren't all that glamorous. You don't have to solve world hunger to make a worthy contribution (though it'd be cool if you did.) It's enough to make lots of small choices that add up to being a good person.

truth be told quotes .com

JOIN US ONLINE FOR:
Journaling Pages
Coloring Pages
Worksheets
Discussion Guides

More from the Author

Colleen Doyle Bryant is the author of five books and more than 50 teaching resources on making good choices for the right reasons, including the Talking with Trees Series for children and Rooted in Decency.

ColleenDoyleBryant.com